PRESENTED BY

Andrew Tague
In Honor of
Mrs. Lamplugh

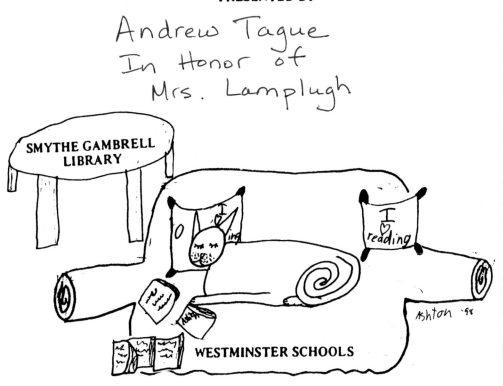

The Boston Tea Party

Laurie A. O'Neill

Spotlight on American History
The Millbrook Press • Brookfield, Connecticut

Cover photograph courtesy of The Granger Collection

Photographs courtesy of The New England (mural by Charles Hoffbauer):
p. 8; The Granger Collection: pp. 13, 28, 33, 40, 48, 56; Bettmann: pp. 15,
18, 45 (left); North Wind Picture Archives: pp. 23, 37; John Carter Brown
Library at Brown University: p. 25; Library of Congress: pp. 30, 50, 55;
Museum of Fine Arts, Boston: p. 45 (right).

Library of Congress Cataloging-in-Publication Data
O'Neill, Laurie, 1949–
The Boston Tea Party / Laurie A. O'Neill
p.   cm.— (Spotlight on American history)
Includes bibliographical references and index.
ISBN 0-7613-0006-6 (lib. bdg.)
1. Boston Tea Party, 1773—Juvenile literature.   I. Title.
II. Series.
E215.7.047   1996
973.3′115—dc20   95-26442   CIP

Published by The Millbrook Press, Inc.
2 Old New Milford Road
Brookfield, Connecticut 06804

Contents

To Nina

The Boston Tea Party

In a mural by Charles Hoffbauer entitled "Tense Meeting at 'Old South' leads to Boston Tea Party, 1773," colonists are shown making speeches and debating their course of action.

One

CRISIS IN BOSTON

*I*t was a raw gray December afternoon in 1773, and a freezing drizzle fell upon the city of Boston, Massachusetts. It was a day to stay indoors and warm, by the fire.

But the people of Boston faced a crisis. Despite the weather, thousands hurried along the narrow, winding streets of the busy seaport. Church bells pealed insistently, urging them toward a simple, white-steepled brick building set in the heart of the city.

Among those rushing to Old South Church was a short, stocky man, his gray wig uncombed and askew, his worn red cape flapping behind him. He was Samuel Adams, leader of the radical cause in Massachusetts, which was protesting England's treatment of its American colonies. Adams's face was set and grim, but his blue eyes fairly danced with excitement.

By 3 P.M. the church, Boston's largest public gathering place, was packed. A restless crowd of nearly 7,000 people spilled out into the street. Their anxious murmuring rose to a fever pitch. Then a gavel fell—once, twice, three times—and the meeting was called to order.

The issue was again presented to the people. Three ships carrying crates of tea from England were tied up at Griffin's Wharf in Boston Harbor. For two weeks Adams and his followers had tried to prevent the tea from being unloaded. Tea was a favorite colonial beverage, but it had become a hated symbol of British oppression. The 342 crates of tea aboard the ships carried a tax of threepence per pound that had been set by Parliament, Britain's governing body.

The tea was to be sold in Boston not by colonial merchants, as it had always been before, but by agents chosen by the East India Company, a British firm. Most of the agents were friends and relatives of Royal governors and judges. It was not the tax—a trifling amount—that the Patriots, as Adams and others loyal to America were known, resented as much as the fact that Parliament had passed the Tea Act without any input from the colonies.

The Patriots wanted a peaceful resolution to the situation. But the threat of violence hung over the city. Thousands of British soldiers—the colonists called them Redcoats—were stationed at Castle Island, a British fortress on an island in Boston Harbor. A pair of British warships rode at anchor nearby.

It was no secret that Boston had been preparing for trouble. Many shopkeepers had sold out their supplies of pistols. "They are all bought up," reported one merchant, "with a full determination to repell [sic] force with force."

Two

FROM RESISTANCE TO REBELLION

Earlier that day Adams had summoned Francis Rotch, a part-owner of the tea ship *Dartmouth*, to a meeting at Old South Church. He ordered Rotch to visit the Royal governor, Thomas Hutchinson, and ask for permission to return the *Dartmouth*'s cargo of tea to England.

Rotch was allowed several hours to make the trip. Due to the trouble that brewed in Boston, the governor had fled to Unkity Hill, his country estate in Milton, some 14 miles (23 kilometers) away. Rotch was to report back to Old South at 3 P.M. If the governor did not grant the shipowner a pass to sail that very day, Royal customs officials would seize and unload the tea and all the Patriots' efforts would have failed.

While the crowd anxiously awaited Rotch's return, several impassioned speeches were made to convince the colonists to take a stand against Britain. Josiah Quincy, a young lawyer, was said to have declared: "I see the clouds now rise thick and fast upon our horizon, the thunder roll, and the lightning play, and to that God who rides the whirlwind and directs the storm, I commit my country!"

Samuel Adams

DESPITE A HARVARD EDUCATION and a sizable inheritance from his father, Samuel Adams, born on September 27, 1722, had no head for business. He was a failure as a merchant, and later as a tax collector, in part because he had difficulty taking money from those as poor as or poorer than he.

But as a politician Adams was a natural. He allied himself with the common people and believed deeply in the right to life, liberty, and property. Persuasive, passionate about the Patriot cause, an effective writer, and a tireless agitator, he could stir up a crowd as few other leaders could.

Adams, second cousin to John Adams, did not look like a radical. A faithful churchgoer, he was soft-spoken, slow-moving, and suffered from a tremor that caused his hands to shake. During the years prior to the Revolution, he would walk around Boston, visiting the places where workers gathered to discuss the issues of the day. He made it a point to know as many people as he could.

Adams served in the First (1774) and Second (1775) Continental Congress and was a signer of the Declaration of Independence. In 1789, in his late sixties, he was elected lieutenant governor (under John Hancock) of Massachusetts. He became governor after Hancock's death in 1793.

Often called "the father of the Revolution," Adams, who died on October 2, 1803, is best remembered for orchestrating the Boston Tea Party and for helping to unite the colonies against British oppression. "With the town meeting," it has been said, "Samuel Adams overthrew an empire."

Samuel Adams was a second cousin of John Adams, who became the second president of the United States in 1796 and who also opposed the British tax on tea.

John Rowe, a prominent merchant, reflected the frustration of the Patriots. "Who knows," he called out, "how tea will mingle with salt water?"

Dusk fell and there was still no sign of Rotch. Someone lit the candles on the wall sconces, and several people carried lanterns, but the light in the meetinghouse was as dim as the hopes the Patriots had for good news from the governor.

At 5:45 P.M., Rotch clattered up to Old South, chilled to the bone from his cold, wet ride. He dismounted and pushed his way into the hall. "The governor," he declared, "has refused to allow my ship to sail with its cargo."

There was an immediate outcry. "A mob!" some in the hall called out, advocating a riot. This was met with cheers. "Order! Order!" cried Adams, rapping the podium. He turned to Rotch. "Will you tell the *Dartmouth* it must return with its cargo to England?" he asked. "I cannot," replied the shipowner, miserably. "It would be the ruin of me."

"Then will you try to unload the tea?" Adams demanded, his voice rising. Rotch hesitated, then answered, "If I am properly called upon to do it." The crowd fell into stunned silence.

Adams took a deep breath. His voice quavering, he proclaimed, *"This meeting can do nothing more to save the country!"*

These ten words from Adams were a signal: A war whoop rose from the gallery and was answered in kind from the front door. Everyone turned to look. There were about fifty men roughly disguised as Mohawk Indians and carrying hatchets. They formed a double column and began marching down Milk Street toward the waterfront.

"Boston Harbor a teapot tonight!" someone shouted inside the hall. Then the crowd surged out and followed the "Indians." So

*Rushing to Griffin's Wharf, a mob of Patriot supporters cheered
as others set out to dump the British tea into the harbor.*

loud was the roar from Old South that people in houses several blocks away ran outside to see what was going on. One, John Andrews, was nearly trampled by the crowd. "You'd have thought that the inhabitants of the infernal regions had broke loose," he said later.

It has been said the Revolutionary War began that night, December 16, 1773, at Griffin's Wharf in Boston, Massachusetts. Finally, years of tension between England and America had come to a head in a simple yet dramatic event that would change the course of history.

Three

TAXATION WITHOUT REPRESENTATION

*B*y *the mid-1700s,* England's thirteen American colonies covered an area of 250,000 square miles (647,500 square kilometers), about three times the size of Britain, and stretched 1,500 miles (2,414 kilometers) up and down the Atlantic coast. The population of the colonies was about 2.5 million, including 500,000 slaves. There were a few major cities, including New York, Philadelphia, and Boston, but most towns were small and far apart. Travel was difficult and sometimes dangerous, and the colonies had limited contact with one another.

Boston, with 17,000 residents, was the capital of the Massachusetts Bay Colony and a prosperous, thriving center of the shipping trade. Beyond its long wharf-lined waterfront were the masts of hundreds of whalers, schooners, and other vessels. Items as exotic as green tea and silk from China, as practical as glass and paper from England, and as popular as West Indies rum were imported by the colony.

In Britain, however, there were increasing financial problems. The French and Indian War, fought for eight years between England and France for control of North America, had been very

*By the mid-1700s, Boston was a bustling port and
capital of the Massachusetts Bay Colony.*

costly. Though the Treaty of Paris in 1763 made Britain a great colonial power (it now claimed the area from the Hudson Bay in the north, the Gulf of Mexico in the south, and the Mississippi River in the west), victory was expensive. The British national debt had doubled to 140 million pounds sterling.

Now Britain needed money to pay its war debts and to defend its newly expanded empire. Already British subjects were the most heavily taxed in the world. England turned to the American colonies, passing a series of new tax laws and toughening the enforcement of existing laws. By doing this the government also wanted to remind the colonists that they were still dependent on and controlled by their mother country.

The colonists, who had begun settling in America in the early 1600s, had at first been grateful for British support and protection in the New World. For the first 100 years, there had been minimal interference from England, mostly because the colonies were so far away.

As a result, they had begun to think of themselves as Americans, with a separate identity from Britain. During the French and Indian War they had raised their own militia and found that they could defend themselves more than successfully. Their system of self-government, though overseen by Britain, worked well.

Each colony was separately governed and had its own legislative body, called the Assembly. This group passed laws and decided taxes. Qualified voters—white male property owners—could participate in town meetings and elect Assembly members.

The king, however, appointed governors and judges for the colonies and had the power to veto any laws passed there. Many colonists were Tories, members of the conservative political party that remained loyal to the Crown. George III, who became king

Today's Living History

BOSTON'S RICH COLONIAL HISTORY can be recalled on nearly every street corner.

At the Old South Meeting House interpretive material about the Boston Tea Party is available to visitors, who can listen to a tape that reconstructs the fiery debates leading to the destruction of the tea.

Tea salvaged from the Boston Tea Party is on display in the collections of the Old South Meeting House, the Old State House, and the Old North Church museums. At the Boston Tea Party Ship and Museum, which boasts a full-scale replica of the brig *Beaver*, reenactments of the December 16 town meeting and the Tea Party itself take place daily, and visitors are encouraged to participate.

In front of Faneuil Hall, "the cradle of American Liberty," stands a statue of Samuel Adams. A circle of cobblestones across from the Old State House marks the site of the Boston Massacre. Paul Revere's house is still standing, the oldest wooden structure in Boston. The graves of Patriots Samuel Adams, John Hancock, Paul Revere, and the victims of the Boston Massacre can be visited in the Granary Burial Ground near the Common.

Griffin's Wharf no longer exists. But on its site at the corner of Atlantic Avenue and Pearl Street is a plaque honoring the place "where about ninety citizens of Boston, partly disguised as Indians, boarded the ships, threw the cargoes, three hundred and forty two chests in all, into the sea, and made the world ring with the exploit of the Boston Tea Party."

in 1760 at the age of twenty-two, was a stubborn ruler and fiercely devoted to both his family and his country. He would fail to acknowledge, until it was too late, the extent of discontent in the American colonies.

When Britain began coming down hard on America, the colonists became angry and resentful. The Whig party, whose members supported reform and colonial independence, grew in popularity as opposition to British control grew. The colonists had no say in Parliament's new tax laws. They could not even elect people to change them. When they asked the British government to listen to their grievances, their requests were ignored. A cry would soon be heard: "Taxation without representation is tyranny."

Four

STAMP ACT PROTESTS

The first organized colonial protests against the new tax laws took place in 1764. George Grenville, the British prime minister, had introduced an act that reinforced previous molasses (sugar) taxes, which had been largely ignored.

Customs officials, who had been allowed to live in England, would now be posted in America and would be dealing with the colonies directly. And the number of British ships along the Atlantic coast would be increased. The colonists held meetings to protest the Sugar Act. "If taxes are laid upon us without our being represented in Parliament," Adams was said to have declared at one gathering, "are we not reduced from free subjects to slaves?"

Though resentful, the colonists paid the taxes. Then, only months after the Sugar Act became law, Britain announced another scheme to raise money in America. Parliament had approved sending 10,000 British troops to the new American frontier, and the colonies were to pay a portion of the cost, which was about 100,000 pounds sterling.

The law called for a stamp to be affixed to some fifty paper items, including all legal documents. The stamps would cost from

Meetings of the Sons of Liberty were punctuated by angry speeches against Britain's unfair tax practices.

a half penny to 10 pounds sterling each, and had to be paid for in cash. Violators would face fines or arrest. Nearly every form of paper used in the colonies was subject to the tax: newspapers, deeds, insurance policies, mortgages, marriage certificates, diplomas— even playing cards.

Word of the Stamp Act reached the colonies in May 1765, six months before the law would take effect. Many colonists were incensed. Why should they continue to pay Britain's war debt when they had already contributed aid and military support?

In Virginia, Patrick Henry, a lawyer and powerful orator, proposed several resolutions condemning the Stamp Act. The document was circulated throughout the colonies. In Boston, Adams and his followers proposed a boycott. Among the group was Paul Revere, a veteran of the French and Indian War and a prominent silversmith and engraver.

Merchants were told to stop buying and selling British goods. Smuggling, already a thriving practice, increased. British manufacturers and workers began feeling the colonists' wrath as stock piled up in British warehouses.

A stamp in the image of a skull and crossbones appeared in colonial newspapers as a symbol of American indignation. Agents who had been appointed to collect the tax were threatened and sometimes beaten.

Adams and his followers were behind nearly every protest. They took rival street gangs from North and South Boston and channeled their anger into the Patriot cause. The Sons of Liberty, as this secret organization was known, soon had chapters throughout the colonies. Its members ordered the stamp collectors to resign or face the consequences, which included tarring and feathering.

The practice was horrible. Boiling tar was poured all over the victim. The gooey, burning mess could cause permanent scars and possibly blindness. Then a pillow was ripped open and the contents scattered over the victim. Finally, he was made to straddle a fence rail, and was carried out of town and dumped into a ditch. Just the threat of tar and feathers was usually enough to get an agent to cooperate.

In August 1765, the office and gracious Boston home of tax agent Andrew Oliver was ransacked. Oliver was hanged in effigy

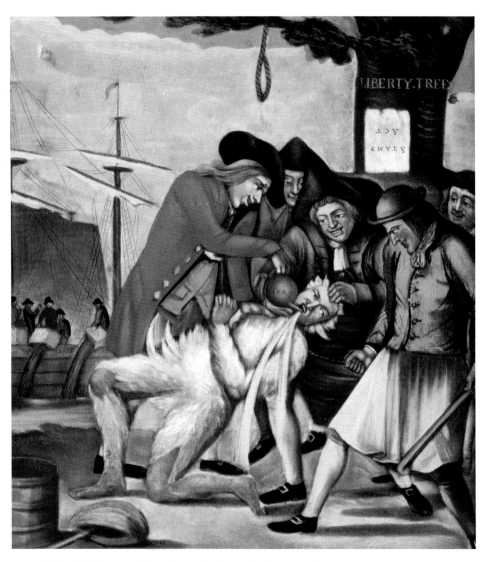

*This 1774 engraving shows jeering colonists forcing tea down the throat
of a British tax collector whom they have just tarred and feathered.
In the background is the Liberty Tree and "tea party" in progress.*

from a towering elm tree in Hanover Square. "What greater joy did New England see/ Than a stampman hanging in a tree," read the note pinned to Oliver's likeness. Named the Liberty Tree, the elm would become the site of many anti-British protests.

Later that month the home of Thomas Hutchinson, then the colony's lieutenant governor, was nearly destroyed and most of his belongings stolen, an act of vandalism that left many Bostonians ashamed and that even Adams regretted.

The Daughters of Liberty were organized during this time. Their protests, however, were nonviolent. These colonial women worked to support the boycotts, shunning imported fabrics, for example, and producing their own homespun cloth.

In October delegates from nine of the thirteen colonies met in New York to discuss the Stamp Act. It was the first gathering of colonial representatives to be held without the permission of the British government. The Stamp Act Congress lasted two weeks and produced a declaration of colonial rights and a petition to Parliament demanding repeal of the law.

With the help of Benjamin Franklin, a colonial agent posted in England to keep the colonists informed of parliamentary activity, the Stamp Act was repealed in March 1766. In America there was dancing in the streets and a public observance of King George's twenty-eighth birthday in May.

But Adams saw no reason to celebrate. While repealing the Stamp Act, Parliament had passed the Declaratory Act. Stating that the British government could continue to make laws affecting America, it reasserted England's power over the colonies. The Stamp Act protests united the colonies against British injustice. This would prove valuable, for it would not be long before England again would bring its heavy hand down on America.

Five

BLOOD IN THE SNOW

harles Townshend, British chancellor of the exchequer, had an idea. He proposed placing heavy duties on a number of English goods exported to the colonies. They included paper, paint, lead, glass, and tea. The Townshend Acts would become law on November 20, 1767.

Though quiet had prevailed for more than a year, Boston again erupted into protests. The Patriots launched another boycott, threatening any merchant who did not cooperate. Under the new law general search warrants called writs of assistance could be used in the colonies to locate smuggled goods. With a writ, customs officials could enter any building, including a private home, and conduct a search, a practice that was illegal in England. The colonists were furious.

Nearly every household felt the effects of the Townshend Acts. Americans loved tea as much as did the British. But many colonists either stopped using the beverage or procured tea smuggled from Holland. Some began brewing coffee.

The Townshend Acts created such an uproar that Parliament felt it needed to provide a show of British strength in the colonies.

British troops landed in Boston on October 1, 1768,
to enforce the Townshend Acts.

In the fall of 1768, troops, 1,000 to start, began arriving in Boston. They marched up from the waterfront, pitched their tents on Boston Common, and occupied public and private buildings, including the Old State House, the center of colonial government.

Suddenly there were Redcoats everywhere, one for every four or five Bostonians. They patrolled the streets, harassed pedestrians, exercised their horses on the Common, and spent the evenings noisily relaxing in the taverns. They neither understood nor respected the colonial way of life, often ridiculing the colonists by singing "Yankee Doodle" in a mocking way.

For their part, the colonists did not trust the Redcoats. They taunted them as they passed in their red and white uniforms and called them "Lobsterbacks." Tension mounted and fistfights were commonplace.

On a cold, clear night in March 1770, Boston lay under several inches of snow. The streets were dark (the city had no streetlights yet) and icy as British Captain John Goldfinch walked past the Royal Customs House. He was followed by two young men. One, Edward Garrick, was a Boston wigmaker's apprentice. He began harassing the officer about an unpaid bill.

Private Hugh White was on duty in a sentry box. He came to Captain Goldfinch's defense, striking Garrick on the side of the head with his musket. Garrick howled and ran off, returning in minutes with several friends, some of them carrying clubs. Soon about fifty colonists surrounded the sentry, hurling insults and snowballs imbedded with stones.

White tried to back up the steps into the Customs House, but he could not get in. Frightened, he called for help: "Turn out, Main Guard!" he cried. Captain Thomas Preston and seven other soldiers emerged from the Old State House and tried to form a line between the mob and the sentry. They, too, were pelted with chunks of ice and snow. Ringing church bells alerted the townspeople to trouble. They rushed from their houses, thinking there was a fire.

"Kill the Bloodybacks!" the crowd shouted. "Fire, you cowards!" The British had been told not to fire at the colonists without

On March 1, 1770, the Boston Massacre resulted in the deaths of five colonists. This engraving, which made it look as if the British were attacking unarmed Patriots, was printed and sold by Paul Revere.

an order from the Royal governor. But it was dark, and in the confusion a soldier was struck with a club. Shots rang out, and in moments five colonists lay dead or dying. The first to fall was Crispus Attucks, a runaway slave who worked on the docks.

It was over quickly. Preston and his men retreated into the guardhouse. The crowd dispersed. By morning the soldiers were in jail, and Preston was charged with murder. Adams was thoroughly outraged. He chose to see the confrontation not as a street fight provoked by Bostonians, which it was, but as a clear example of British aggression.

Broadsides (large sheets of paper printed on one side) were circulated within hours, calling the incident a "massacre." Decidedly biased engravings of the event showed unarmed townspeople being fired upon mercilessly by a line of Redcoats.

Although they were ardent Patriots, John Adams, a lawyer and second cousin of Samuel Adams, and Josiah Quincy defended the soldiers, insisting that they deserved a fair trial. Preston and six soldiers were found not guilty. The remaining two men were found guilty of manslaughter. They were branded on their thumbs with a hot iron and released.

Bostonians demanded that the troops leave the city, and the soldiers were removed to Castle William. Ironically, March 5, 1770, was not only the date of the Boston Massacre. It was also the day that it was proposed that Parliament repeal the Townshend Acts, with one exception. There would still be a tax on tea.

Six

THAT PESTILENT BRITISH HERB

At first the tea tax failed to draw major opposition. It is important to know that not all the people in the colonies supported the Patriot cause. Roughly a third were Tories, and another third took a neutral position, fearing it was too dangerous to protest against Britain. Most of the Patriots refused to drink the beverage, but some continued to obtain smuggled tea. Adams's radicals tried to keep the resistance movement alive. They hoped to convince the colonies to become a unified America.

To that end Adams formed the first Committee of Correspondence in the fall of 1772. Its twenty-one members wrote letters to inform people in other towns and colonies of the latest British injustice or Patriot protest. Similar committees were set up in other towns (by January 1773, there were eighty committees in Massachusetts) and in distant colonies. Virginia's committee counted among its members Thomas Jefferson, a lawyer and wealthy landowner. Within months, these committees would have plenty to write about.

The East India Company had been one of the largest and most powerful firms in England. Its chief export was tea. Buying

The British East India Company in London was a successful business in the seventeenth century. By the 1770s it was nearly bankrupt and had turned to the British government for help in selling its stockpiles of tea.

its tea leaves directly from Canton in China, the company had been selling more than 4 million pounds (1.8 million kilograms) of tea a year. By the early 1770s the company faced bankruptcy due to poor management, American boycotts, and active smuggling of tea both by Britain and by its colonies.

So much tea—17 million pounds (7.7 million kilograms)—had piled up in English warehouses that the company turned to the government for help. Parliament was quick to respond, in large part because several of its members had invested heavily in the tea company.

The British government conceived a plan that would save the company, dispose of its overstocks, and make money as well. The firm would be given a monopoly on the tea trade in America. That is, it could sell its tea directly to the colonies, without paying an export tax, through its own agents, or consignees. These consignees would be Tories. Because no colonial merchants could deal in tea, they would be put out of business.

The price of the tea would be so low, even lower than smuggled tea, that British officials were certain that the colonists would not complain about the threepence tax that would be added to its price.

The plan was masterminded by the British prime minister, Frederick Lord North, with the enthusiastic support of King George. "I am clear there must always be one tax to keep the right and as such I approve the Tea Duty," he declared.

In Boston, five tea consignees were selected to collect the tax and pay it to the British government. The East India Company would prepare to ship a total of 600,000 pounds (272,160 kilograms) of tea to Boston, New York, Philadelphia, and Charleston, South Carolina.

The Tea Act went into effect on May 10, 1773. When the colonies learned of the new law, it stirred them up as nothing had before. Again, cries of "taxation without representation" echoed up and down the Atlantic seacoast. Colonial merchants feared the British government would extend this kind of monopoly to other goods. Samuel and John Adams, Paul Revere, and John Hancock, a wealthy Bostonian who underwrote many of the radicals' activities, sprang into action.

Meetings were called, the committees of correspondence generated a flurry of letters, and the Sons of Liberty renewed their campaign of threats and harassment. Tea became the symbol of British oppression, and a boycott was begun. Anti-tea leagues were organized by women who referred to the tea as "that pestilent British herb."

This time the boycott was widely honored, at great sacrifice. Not only was tea believed to have restorative and curative powers, but teatime was a ritual among all classes of colonists. It was a time for relaxation and pleasant conversation. Many households possessed elaborate silver or porcelain tea services: tray, pot, stand, cups and saucers, creamer, sugar bowl, spoons, tongs, tea caddy, and urn. It is estimated that 6.5 million pounds (3 million kilograms) of tea were consumed each year in America. A third of Boston's residents were said to drink it twice a day.

In late September 1773, seven ships sailed down the Thames River from London and awaited good weather. On October 18 they entered the open Atlantic. The East India Company had no idea that the vessels might encounter problems on the other side of the ocean.

The ships carried a total of nearly 2,000 wooden chests filled with tightly packed tea leaves wrapped in canvas. Each lead-lined chest, called a tare, could weigh nearly 400 pounds (182 kilograms) when full. There was Hyson, a choice, green tea, carefully packed in half or quarter tares. The rest was black tea, some of it singlo and souchong, but the bulk of it was bohea (bo-HEE), the most common and least expensive leaves.

Bound for Boston were the *Dartmouth*, the *Eleanor*, and the *Beaver*, each holding 114 tares, and the *William*, with 58. The largest shipment of tea, 698 chests, was aboard the *Nancy*, headed for New York. Six hundred tares were in the *Polly*'s hold, en route to Philadelphia. And the *London* carried 257 chests bound for the port of Charleston.

The captain of each ship was required by law to report immediately to the customshouse upon arrival, then unload the ship's cargo at the wharf. Failure to do this was punishable by a sizable fine. If the duties on the cargo were not paid within twenty days after arrival, the goods could be seized by customs officials.

Opposition came first in New York and Philadelphia, where handbills alerted colonists to the ships' approach. The consignees were threatened with violence. By October, the agents in all the ports except Boston had resigned. The approaching ships were given warning. The *Polly* received this message from the Sons of Liberty in Philadelphia: "What think you Captain, of a Halter around your Neck, then Gallons of liquid Tar decanted on your Pate [head] with the Feathers of a dozen live Geese laid over that to enliven your appearance?"

This handbill from the Committee for Tarring and Feathering in Philadelphia called the captain of the tea ship Polly *a "short, fat fellow."*

TO THE

DELAWARE
PILOTS.

THE Regard we have for your Characters, and our Defire to promote your future Peace and Safety, are the Occafion of this Third Addrefs to you

IN our fecond Letter we acquainted you, that the Tea Ship was a Three Decker ; We are now informed by good Authority, fhe is not a Three Decker, but an *old black Ship, without a Head,* or *any Ornaments.*

THE *Captain* is a *fhort fat* Fellow, and a little *obftinate* withal — So much the worfe for him ....For, fo fure as he *rides rufty,* We fhall heave him Keel out, and fee that his Bottom be well fired, fcrubb'd and paid,— His Upper-Works too, will have an Overhawling. — and as it is faid, he has a good deal of *Quick Work* about him, We will take particular Care that fuch Part of him undergoes a thorough Rummaging

WE have a ftill *worfe Account* of his *Owner,*— for it is faid, the Ship POLLY was bought by him on Purpofe, to make a Penny of us , and that *he* and Captain *Ayres* were well advifed of the Rifque they would run, in thus daring to infult and abufe us.

Captain Ayres was here in the Time of the Stamp-Act, and ought to have known our People better, than to have expected we would be fo mean as to fuffer his *rotten* TEA to be funnel'd down our Throats, with the *Parliament's Duty* mixed with it.

WE know him well, and have calculated to a Gill and a Feather, how much it will require to fit him for an *American Exhibition.* And we hope, not one of your Body will behave fo ill, as to oblige us to clap him in the Cart along Side of the *Captain,*

WE muft repeat, that the SHIP POLLY is an *old black Ship,* of about Two Hundred and Fifty Tons burthen *without a Head,* and *without Ornaments,*— and, that CAPTAIN AYRES is a *thick chunky Fellow.*........— As fuch, TAKE CARE to AVOID THEM.

YOUR OLD FRIENDS,

THE COMMITTEE FOR TARRING AND FEATHERING

Philadelphia, December 7, 1773.

In Charleston, South Carolina, the tea was unloaded but stored in a warehouse. Though it was reported that the tea was allowed to rot, it was actually sold at auction two years later to help the Continental Army. All of the ships except those bound for Boston returned to England.

Seven

THE FLAME IS KINDLED

The situation was especially tense in Massachusetts. Hutchinson, now the Royal governor, was a staunch Loyalist (one who is faithful to the Crown) and an investor in the East India Company. Two of his sons, Elisha and Thomas, Jr., were consignees. Already the city was becoming a hotbed of anti-British sentiment, thanks to the work of Samuel Adams and his fellow agitators.

Hutchinson was alarmed at the growing unrest around him. In November he sent word to England: "At present the spirits of the people in the town of Boston are in great ferment."

Huge meetings were held nearly every day in Boston's Faneuil Hall, above the public marketplace. They were not official town meetings, which only qualified voters could attend, but gatherings of what came to be called the Body—any people from Boston and beyond who were interested in attending.

For weeks the Patriots pressured the shipowners to return the tea to England and the five consignees to resign. In any case, the Body resolved to prevent the landing of the tea. The number and frequency of these meetings reflect the Patriots' struggle to settle the crisis peacefully.

Faneuil Hall in Boston was the site of huge meetings held to discuss what could be done to prevent the landing of the British tea ships.

During the night of November 2 handbills were posted all over Boston, requesting "the Freemen of this and neighboring Towns" to witness the consignees resign their posts at noon the next day, under the Liberty Tree. Summonses were prepared for the five agents and delivered before dawn. By 11 A.M. church bells began to peal and town criers roamed Boston's streets, calling the people to the meeting.

More than five hundred colonists assembled under the great elm. Samuel Adams, John Hancock, and Dr. Joseph Warren, another Patriot, spoke to the crowd. The consignees had refused to attend the meeting and had gathered instead at a warehouse on Long Wharf. There was a chorus of angry shouting and booing.

Adams held up his hand for silence. "Do we agree the agents must resign?" he asked. The people cheered. "And if they refuse, can we call them enemies of America?" he added. The crowd roared.

A delegation was sent to the warehouse to request the agents' resignations. Dozens of Bostonians followed. The leader of the group, William Molineux, knocked at the warehouse door and called for the agents to resign. There was no response. The delegation turned to leave, but several Bostonians began pounding on the door and trying to break into the building. Molineux ordered them to disperse. Inside, the five consignees were shaken and afraid.

On November 17, word arrived that the tea ships were only a few days out of Boston. Again the Patriots asked the consignees to abandon their positions. The five agents turned to Hutchinson for help. "Will you take the tea under government protection?" they asked him.

The governor refused, but assured them that there would be no violence. "Customs will simply seize the tea after twenty days," he said, "and Adams and his rabblerousers will have lost." This did little to calm the men, so Hutchinson advised them to take refuge with their families at Castle William. Meanwhile Adams's resistance movement was gaining support from afar. "Stand firm, Boston!" urged the committees of correspondence in New York and Philadelphia.

On Sunday, November 28, the *Dartmouth*, the first of the tea ships, arrived. The next morning the city was covered with handbills. "FRIENDS! BRETHREN! GENTLEMEN! That worst of plagues, the detested TEA . . . has now arrived. . . . Every friend to his country, to his posterity, is now called upon to meet at Faneuil Hall at nine o'clock THIS DAY to make a united and successful resistance to this last, worst, and most destructive measure of the Administration."

Boston buzzed with excitement. Again bells rang out wildly and people streamed to Faneuil Hall—5,000 of them. Adams announced the arrival of the *Dartmouth* and proposed a resolution: "that the tea . . . be returned to the place from whence it came." The crowd's response was deafening.

A guard made up of twenty-five volunteers, mostly Sons of Liberty, was posted at Griffin's Wharf. Armed with muskets, the men made sure the ships were not unloaded. For the next two weeks calls of "All's well" floated in the darkness along the wharf. Even Paul Revere and John Hancock took their turns on watch.

On November 30, Hutchinson sent word from Unkity Hill to the Patriots gathered at yet another meeting: "Your actions are illegal." He ordered them to disperse. Though the Patriots knew that what they were doing amounted to treason in the eyes of the British government, they responded to the order with boos and hisses.

The *Eleanor* tied up at Griffin's Wharf on December 1 or 2. The *Beaver* would not arrive until December 15. Smallpox had been discovered aboard the ship, and it had to be quarantined for a week on an island in the harbor while its hold was fumigated with smoke. The *William* never made it to Boston. On December 10 it was wrecked in a storm at Provincetown on Cape Cod. Its cargo, including three hundred of what would be Boston's first street lamps, was salvaged. The tea was likely sold later to Tories.

Hundreds of townspeople flocked to the wharf to gawk at the ships and wonder aloud what would happen. Abigail Adams, the wife of John Adams, sent a letter to her close friend, writer Mercy Otis Warren, who lived in Plymouth. "The tea, that baneful weed, is arrived . . ." she wrote. "The flame is kindled and like lightning it catches from soul to soul."

The governor was determined to uphold Royal law. If he allowed the ships to sail with the tea, it would be an admission of defeat. Hutchinson ordered the British naval commander, Admiral Montagu, to anchor two British warships at the outer harbor.

The Body was in nearly constant session from December 14 to December 16. Rotch was ordered to request clearance from the customshouse to sail. This was denied. Handbills warned that anyone caught unloading the tea would be punished. The shipowners, concerned about the fate of their vessels and cargo, protested to the governor. It was expensive to remain in port and pay wages to their crews, they said.

John Singleton Copley, the great portraitist and the son-in-law of a consignee, rowed out to Castle William to speak with the agents and plead with them to return to Boston. They refused. When Copley returned, he begged the Patriots not to harm the consignees, but his words were drowned out by angry shouting. Anger and frustration mounted on both sides. A showdown was obviously coming.

Pioneer Feminists

EIGHTEENTH-CENTURY WOMEN had little, if any, voice in politics and rarely played a part in public life. But two Massachusetts residents were exceptions to that rule.

Born in 1744, ABIGAIL ADAMS, daughter of a Weymouth minister, had been exposed to ideas and issues that at the time were usually reserved for men. She was a gifted letter writer who corresponded frequently with her husband, John, a lawyer, while he was away on business, and with her close friend Mercy Otis Warren. These letters provide valuable background material on Revolutionary War-era Massachusetts.

Adams spent nearly ten years managing her family farm alone. Her five children included John Quincy Adams, who became the sixth president of the United States. A confidante to her husband throughout his long public career, which culminated in the U.S. presidency, Adams often drew criticism from his political opponents. She continually urged him to include women in government—advice that Adams largely ignored.

"Remember the ladies . . ." she once wrote him. "Do not put such unlimited power into the hands of the husbands." Abigail, who died in 1818, is considered to be the first advocate for women's rights in America.

MERCY OTIS WARREN, born in Barnstable in 1728, was the sister of the radical James Otis, the wife of Revolutionary leader James Warren, and the mother of five children. She was an intellectual, a wit, an avid reader, and a gifted writer. Warren corres-

Abigail Adams (left) and Mercy Otis Warren (right)

ponded with several prominent American leaders, including Thomas Jefferson and George Washington, and with Abigail Adams.

Openly sympathetic to the Patriot cause, she wrote several propagandist pamphlets, as well as a number of poems and plays. Her three-volume eyewitness account of the Revolutionary War, published in 1805, is one of the most important colonial histories ever written. An early feminist, Warren believed that women deserved an education equal to that received by men. She died in 1814.

Eight

SALTWATER TEA

While the crowd at Old South Church waited for Rotch to return, other Patriots had been gathering all afternoon in various locations around Boston. Adams and his followers had prepared a plan of action in case the news from the governor was not good.

The plan and its participants were shrouded in secrecy. In a tavern near the wharf, at the homes of colonists Joseph Shed and Nathanial Bradlee, and in the back of Benjamin Edes's printing office, the men disguised themselves in old, torn clothing and woolen caps, and wrapped themselves in shabby blankets. They smudged their faces with lampblack and chimney soot and carried hatchets. The men referred to themselves as Mohawks. However, contrary to artists' renderings of the day, they did not wear Indian garb or feathered headdresses.

Sarah Bradlee Fulton helped her husband, John, and several other men, with their disguises. At Edes's office, Benjamin's young son Peter made punch for the men, but he was told to stay in the next room so that he could not see who they were.

When the "Indians" set out for Griffin's Wharf from Old South, it was clear that this was not a spontaneous act but rather a well-conceived plan. As they marched in silence toward the waterfront, they were joined by dozens more colonists who wanted to take part in the rebellion. When the group reached the wharf, the rain had ceased, but the weather was raw and windy. Swiftly moving storm clouds revealed a bright moon, which illuminated the scene. The Patriot guards allowed the men, now numbering about one hundred, to pass, and the "Indians" split into three groups, each with a leader.

They boarded the *Dartmouth*, the *Eleanor*, and the *Beaver* and asked each ship's mate for the keys to the hold and some candles. Then they ordered the crew to go below, assuring them that no one would be hurt and that no damage would be done to the vessels. The sailors did not resist; a few, it is said, may have even helped the Patriots.

Once the holds were unlocked some men went below, and, using block and tackle, hoisted the chests onto the deck. Then others carried them to the rail and split them open. The groups worked quickly and efficiently. All that was heard were the sounds of winches creaking and wood splitting, and the splash of the debris as it hit the water.

"We used no more words than were absolutely necessary," recalled Joshua Wyeth, an apprentice blacksmith who helped dump the tea. "I never worked harder in my life."

The tide was dead low and the water so shallow—less than 2 feet (60 centimeters) deep—that the tea mounded up to the rails. Men stood in the water and pushed the tea down and away from the ships. A crowd of spectators watched in eerie silence on the docks. Oddly, neither the two British warships, only a few hundred yards away, nor the soldiers at Castle William did anything to stop the Patriots.

Although this engraving shows the Patriots dressed as Indians as they tore into the tea and dumped it overboard, it is generally believed that they did not, in fact, actually wear headdresses.

In less than three hours it was over. A brass padlock, which had been broken, was replaced, and there was only one injury, when a Patriot was struck by a piece of hoisting equipment and knocked unconscious. The decks were swept clean, everything was put back in its place, and the first mates were summoned to verify that the ships were not damaged.

Then each group leader ordered his men to remove their shoes and dump any tea leaves that had collected in them over the rail. At least one participant was caught filling his boots, pockets, and coat linings with tea. He was tossed into the crowd, where he was kicked and shoved as he made his way from the ship.

Tea floated on the water as far as you could see. Some 90,000 pounds (41,000 kilograms) of it, worth 10,000 pounds sterling ($33,000 in 1773, $1.8 million today) had been destroyed. The Patriots formed a double line, led by Captain Lendall Pitts. Accompanied by a fifer playing "Yankee Doodle," they shouldered their axes and marched through the parting crowd and into the night.

As they passed a known Tory house, Admiral Montagu appeared in a window. "Well, boys, you've had a fine pleasant evening for your Indian caper, haven't you," he said. "But mind. You have got to pay the fiddler yet!" Captain Pitts was quick with a reply: "Never mind, squire! Just come out here if you please and we'll settle the bill in two minutes!" Montagu, eyebrows raised, slammed the window shut.

The "Indians" disbanded and slipped home. By 10 P.M. there was no sign that the Boston Tea Party, as it would come to be known, had ever taken place. When Joseph Palmer, a hardware merchant, entered his house, his wife screamed. "Don't be frightened, Betsy. It is I," he said. "We've been making a bit of saltwater tea."

The next day the Patriots toasted each other in the taverns and sang a new tune: "Rally, Mohawks!/ Bring out your axes/ Let's tell King George/ We'll pay no taxes!" The *Boston Gazette* trumpeted: "The people are almost universally congratulating each other on this happy event."

The Patriots' rebellion proved to be too much for Governor Hutchinson, who resigned in the midst of the uprising of 1774.

John Adams recorded the following in his diary: "This is the most magnificent movement of all. There is a Dignity, a Majesty, a Sublimity in this last Effort of the Patriots that I greatly admire . . . this destruction of the tea is so bold, so daring, so firm, intrepid and inflexible, and it must have important consequences, and so lasting that I cannot but consider it as an epoch in history."

The consignees stayed on Castle William, because they continued to incur the Patriots' anger. Handbills referred to the agents as "odious miscreants, detestable tools to Ministry and traitors," and the five were warned that, should they return to town, they would be tarred and feathered.

Samuel Adams suggested that news of the destruction of the tea be carried by a messenger to New York and Philadelphia. Paul Revere was chosen to ride, and Adams prepared a dispatch. "Our enemies must acknowledge that these people have acted upon pure and upright principle," it read in part. "We are in perfect jubilee."

Governor Hutchinson was stunned and furious. Montagu told him that the British did not try to stop the proceedings because any military reponse might have resulted in the injury or death of innocent people and serious damage to the harbor.

Now the governor faced humiliation. He would have to inform Parliament and the East India Company of the destruction of the tea. Realizing his authority was now undermined, and that the Patriots hated him, he asked to be relieved of his position.

Nine

BOSTON IS PUNISHED

Word of the tea party reached England with the arrival of a merchant ship on or about January 19, 1774. King George was incredulous, Parliament was insulted, and East India Company officials were astounded; they had lost a fortune in tea.

Cries of "anarchy" resounded across Britain. The incident could not be ignored. Boston, the British government decided, must be punished. An editorial in a London paper reflected the nation's rage: "It would be best to blow the town of BOSTON about the ears of its inhabitants and to destroy that nest of locusts."

Various proposals were made to bring the colonies into line. The government focused on Boston, which it felt was responsible for inciting the colonies to opposition and unrest. Samuel Adams and John Hancock were targeted as traitors. Those who destroyed the tea were to be found and arrested.

But the identities of the perpetrators had been kept a closely guarded secret. For many years an accurate list of participants was impossible to obtain. Among those certain to have taken part were Paul Revere, William Molineux, and Thomas Melville, grandfather of the writer Herman Melville. Samuel Adams and John Hancock stayed behind, possibly to carry out a contingency plan should the tea party go awry.

In March, Lord North proposed a series of harsh measures known as the Coercive Acts. In America they were referred to as the Intolerable Acts. The Port Act called for Boston Harbor to be closed to all trade as of June 1 unless Massachusetts paid for the tea and the tax on it.

Thousands of British troops and four warships were sent to Boston, with orders to fire on any ship attempting to pass Castle William. Parliament also ruled that any serious lawbreakers in the colonies would now be tried in England. The colony's system of self-government was virtually abolished. Town meetings were to be held only with the governor's permission. The capital of Massachusetts was moved to Salem and its customshouse to Plymouth.

General Thomas Gage, a former commander in chief of the British forces in America, replaced Hutchinson as governor of the colony. Not all members of Parliament felt that Boston and the other colonies would back down in the face of a British show of strength. "I believe England will be conquered some day or other in New England," said one, Horace Walpole. His words proved to be prophetic.

Across the ocean the colonists fumed. To be occupied again by the British Army was particularly offensive. Immediately Samuel Adams called for colonial unity. Revere rode south with a copy of the despised Port Act and returned with the news that Patriots in the other colonies were shocked, angry, and ready to support Boston.

Virginia proposed holding a meeting with representatives from all the colonies to discuss the matter. A South Carolina newspaper ran black borders of mourning on June 1, the day the port was closed, and the words "Rise patriotism! To the aid of our much injured country!" Newspapers in New York and New Jersey carried a symbol of a segmented snake, each segment a colony, and the words JOIN OR DIE. Boston's cause had become America's cause.

On September 5, in Philadelphia's Carpenters' Hall, representatives from all thirteen colonies except Georgia, a Tory stronghold, gathered to hold the First Continental Congress. The fifty-six participants included Samuel and John Adams, Thomas Jefferson, Patrick Henry, John Jay, and George Washington—some of the most powerful and respected men in America.

Over the next five weeks they drew up a list of grievances, agreed to a general boycott of British goods until the Intolerable Acts were lifted, and pledged to stand united if force was used against Massachusetts. There was talk of war, but the group vowed that America would not be the one to start it. The Congress sent its resolutions to the king. He responded by sending more warships to the colonies.

While the Philadelphia meetings were in session, Massachusetts was readying its militia. Every able male aged sixteen (and sometimes younger) to sixty was a member. Each had to provide and care for a musket or rifle, powder horn, blanket, and knapsack. The men came from all walks of life; there were sailors, laborers, farmers, and freed slaves, and slaves who were promised their freedom in exchange for their service. Many of the militiamen had fought in the French and Indian War.

The militia trained through the late summer and into the fall, drilling on town greens and open fields. Ammunition was stored in certain towns outside Boston, including Concord. A vital part of the militia was a group of volunteers called the Minutemen, so named because they could be ready at a minute's notice.

Some of the most powerful men in America came away from the September meetings at Carpenters' Hall in Philadelphia determined to fight the Intolerable Acts.

The British watched as the colonial militia took shape. They sent word to their government, which, curiously, seemed unconcerned. Governor Gage, however, was beginning to worry that Britain had been too harsh with the Massachusetts colonists. "It is a great folly," he wrote to England, "which I fear the people will resist to the death, and soon."

This lithograph by Currier & Ives shows a messenger on horseback recruiting volunteers from their homes to join the Minutemen.

Gage devised a plan to prevent an uprising. He would lead an expedition from Boston to Concord to seize arms and ammunition and to find Adams and Hancock, who were said to be staying in the area.

He called for reinforcements, and the operation was set for mid-April.

But the Patriots found out and prepared their own plan. Revere and other messengers rode through the night on April 18, 1775, toward Lexington and Concord. "The Regulars are out!" they cried, warning the countryside of the approach of British troops.

By dawn, seventy or so colonial militiamen stood quietly, in loose formation, on the green at Lexington. Soon a line of Redcoats appeared, marching stiffly to the throbbing of drums and the whistle of a fife. They looked every bit like toy soldiers in their trim crimson, black, and white uniforms with shiny brass and pewter buttons, a sharp contrast to the colonists in their simple homespun shirts and knee britches.

"Disperse, ye rebels!" shouted a British officer. But Captain John Parker, leader of the colonial militia, ordered his men to stand their ground: "If they mean to have a war, let it begin here."

One shot was fired, and then many more. Eight colonists fell dead. Nine were wounded, as were one British soldier and the horse ridden by Major John Pitcairn.

Later some three hundred militiamen and Minutemen intercepted the British at North Bridge in Concord. They routed the Redcoats who, while retreating along the road from Concord to Lexington, were peppered with shots from hundreds more militia and Minutemen hiding behind walls, rocks, and trees. Women fired upon the soldiers from their windows.

Seventy-three British soldiers were killed that day, and close to two hundred more were wounded. The Revolutionary War had begun. It would involve all thirteen colonies and continue for seven years. The destruction of the tea that moonlit December night in Boston Harbor gave the Patriots courage to fight for their freedom. It would lead to the birth of the United States of America.

Chronology

1764   Sugar Act is passed by Parliament.
1765   Stamp Act is passed by Parliament.
1766   Stamp Act is repealed; Declaratory Act is passed.
1767   Townshend Acts are passed by Parliament.
1768   British troops land at Boston.
1770   Townshend Acts repealed, except tax on tea.
        Boston Massacre, March 5.
1773   Tea Act is passed by Parliament.
        Tea Meetings are held at Faneuil Hall, then Old South Church, from early November through mid-December.
        Dartmouth, first of tea ships, anchors in Boston Harbor on November 28.
        All three tea ships dock at Griffin's Wharf by December 15.
        Deadline arrives for taxes to be paid on *Dartmouth*'s tea, December 16.
        Last tea meeting held at Old South Meeting House draws nearly 7,000 people, December 16.
        Boston Tea Party, December 16.
1774   Coercive Acts (Intolerable Acts) are passed by Parliament to punish Boston.
1775   Revolutionary War begins with battles at Lexington and Concord.

Sources

Sources for *The Boston Tea Party* include newspaper articles, diaries, journals, letters, eyewitness accounts, autobiographies, biographies, reference books, and histories of the period. The dialogue in this book appears in several sources used by the author, and either includes actual conversation taken from historical records or what is generally believed to have been said.

Particularly helpful were sources found in the library of The Bostonian Society, the Starr Library at Middlebury College, and the Boston Public Library. The author would like to thank staff members at the Old South Meeting House and the Boston Tea Party Ship and Museum, who patiently answered questions and provided additional materials.

A complete list of sources follows.

Asimov, Isaac. *The Birth of the United States: 1763–1816*. Boston: Houghton Mifflin Company, 1974.

Beller, Susan Provost. *Woman of Independence: The Life of Abigail Adams*. Crozet, Va.: Shoe Tree Press, 1992.

Birnbaum, Louis. *Red Dawn at Lexington*. Boston: Houghton Mifflin Company, 1986.

Brown, Richard D. *Massachusetts: A History*. New York: W. W. Norton & Company, 1978.

Canfield, Cass. *Sam Adams's Revolution*. New York: Harper & Row, 1976.

Coit, Margaret. *Massachusetts*. New York: Coward-McCann, 1967.

Commager, Henry Steele, and Richard B. Morris, eds. *The Spirit of 'Seventy-Six: The Story of the American Revolution as Told by Participants.* New York: Bonanza Books, 1983.

Cushing, Harry Alonzo. *The Writings of Samuel Adams.* Vol. III. 1773–1777. New York: G. P. Putnam's Sons, 1907.

Drake, Francis S. *Tea Leaves.* Boston: A. O. Crane, 1884.

Evans, R. E. *The American War of Independence.* Minneapolis: Lerner Publications Company, 1977.

Fryatt, Norma. *Boston and the Tea Riots.* New York: Auerback, 1972.

Harris, John. "Boston Tea Party: The Trigger of our Revolution." *The Boston Globe,* April 28, 1974.

Kent, Deborah. *The American Revolution: "Give Me Liberty or Give Me Death."* Hillside, N.J.: Enslow Publishers, 1994.

Labaree, Benjamin Woods. *The Boston Tea Party.* New York: Oxford University Press, 1964.

Langguth, A. J. *Patriots: The Men Who Started the American Revolution.* New York: Simon and Schuster, 1988.

Marrin, Albert. *The War for Independence.* New York: Atheneum, 1988.

Meltzer, Milton. *The American Revolutionaries: A History in Their Own Words.* New York: Thomas Y. Crowell, 1987.

Middlekrauff, Robert. *The Glorious Cause: The American Revolution 1763–1789.* New York: Oxford University Press, 1982.

Phelan, Mary Kay. *The Story of the Boston Tea Party.* New York: Thomas Y. Crowell, 1973.

Stearns, Monroe. *The Story of New England.* New York: Random House, 1967.

Stout, Neil R. *The Perfect Crisis: The Beginning of the Revolutionary War.* New York: New York University Press, 1892.

Thomas, Peter D. G. *Tea Party to Independence.* Oxford: Clarendon Press, 1991.

Walett, Francis B. *Patriots, Loyalists and Printers.* Worcester, Mass.: American Antiquarian Society, 1976.

Warren, Mercy Otis. *History of the Rise, Progress and Termination of the American Revolution.* Original publisher, Manning & Loring, Boston, 1805. Reprinted, Indianapolis: Liberty Classics, 1988.

Further Reading

Carter, Alden. *The American Revolution: War for Independence*. New York: Franklin Watts, 1993.

Fritz, Jean. *Can't You Make Them Behave, King George?* New York: Putnam, 1982.

Kent, Deborah. *The American Revolution: "Give Me Liberty, or Give Me Death!"* Hillside, N.J.: Enslow, 1994.

Olesky, Walter. *Boston Tea Party*. New York: Franklin Watts, 1993.

Smith, Carter, ed. *The Revolutionary War: A Sourcebook on Colonial America*. Brookfield, Conn.: The Millbrook Press, 1991.

Steins, Richard. *A Nation Is Born: Rebellion and Independence in America (1700–1820)*. New York: 21st Century Books, 1993.

Index

3